Dear Emma,

Thank you for tuning in and following your hearts call - the animals are with you all the way

love

Anna Breytenbach

xxx

CONTENTS

DEDICATION

This dedication is for all the souls that have been or still are in animal bodies here on Planet Earth. Their ceaseless dedication to assist humanity in waking up to unity consciousness is truly something for us to aspire to and to give eternal gratitude for.

FOREWORD

Today, animal communication is the most powerful tool we humans possess to re-establish a loving and meaningful relationship with the real world. Although this ability dates back from the most ancient times, it is critically relevant to our modern day, and The Key not only to protecting our planet but also to saving ourselves.

That's why Julie Line's inspiring book The Purpose of Species is so important, and so timeous.

The big intelligence test in any family of foreign language speakers is: exactly who's able to learn who's language best? You - or your pet? But while we humans pride ourselves on "training" our household dog, cat, or parrot, in human language, many of us remain impervious to the profound messages these amazing creatures are trying to convey to our species. If only we could hear other species, and view the world from their differing perspectives, we would ourselves become more loving, balanced, healthy and joyous individuals. Julie Lines's elegantly-scribed book shows us that in finding our reconnection with animals, we find ourselves. That's The Key. That's the purpose of species. Her sensitivity to her material - faithfully translating the collective wisdom from each species into human language in a voice that resonates through generations of animal-kind – is a joy and inspiration to anyone yearning to find their souls again, and glimpse the meaning behind creation.

Having spent the last 20 years of my life living with the rare White Lions in the wilds of their natural endemic habitat - the animals regarded by African elders as the 'holiest beasts' on the continent - and receiving messages direct from these kings and queens of animals, I can say with all my heart that species are divinely created: all life is precious, and all Nature sacred. Julie's book allows each species its own unique 'signature-message' for humanity at this time of ecological and psychological crisis: The wise Orang-utans, who withdraw from humankind's ignorance to reflect on the extinction of species: might we only come to know what we've lost once it's gone, and we are dying along with it…?

The bright-sparking cats, "light-takers" who teach us the true law of predation, so different from the brutal, mindless, consumerist killing to which humans subject other species on our planet. The spirited horses, who convey to us the true meaning of freedom; but, like many animal species in these critical times, are no longer prepared to stand the abuse of the old. The exquisitely fine-tuned spiders, who teach us of the dangers and opportunities in the webs we unconsciously weave for ourselves. Overwhelmingly, of all signature-messages, Julie's transmission direct from different animals conveys the deep grief they feel for our species and its sad mistakes, but equally the love and hope they continue to hold in our powers of transformation, and our ability to restore what we have almost lost.

The truth is that each one of us can make a meaningful difference, once we restore the loving and harmonious balance within ourselves. In her book, the wisdom Julie transmits direct from each of the animal species will encourage and guide us to do so – just as animals all around us are encouraging and guiding, always. In reverence and gratitude for all the perspectives that animals have given us, and to Julie for hearing their call.

Linda Tucker
CEO, Global White Lion Protection Trust
Author, Mystery of the White Lions
Mantel Holder, 'Keeper of the White Lions'

ACKNOWLEDGMENTS

I would like to thank first and foremost, Charles and his Grandfather Erasmus Darwin for their tireless persistence, showing up in my life over and over again – showing me that I needed to persist and publish these messages. I would also like to thank all of the guest channelers who kindly submitted their channelled messages, especially to Jean Davies who contributed on more than a few occasions! Thank you to my wonderful partner David William Bell for his constant encouragement and support and thank you to all of my animal family who have always been there for me, those still here and those who have passed over. Thank you to Liz Mitten Ryan for offering her stunning artwork that accompanies some of the messages. A huge thank you to the incredible White Lion protector and ambassador , Linda Tucker, for kindly writing the foreword. Last, but certainly not least, I want to thank all of the animals that have contributed their messages in this book – you are a never ending source of inspiration and wonderful teachings, where would humanity be without you all?

INTRODUCTION

At this point in planetary evolution, humanity is hurtling out of control, consuming far too much of the available resources, with little or no thought of the devastating consequences for the whole planet.

As the one hundred and fiftieth anniversary of the publication of Charles Darwin's "On The Origin of Species" was commemorated in 2010, a consistent calling beckoned me. Knowing a little about Darwin's theories I have always felt there is much more to animals than simply "what" they are physically, much more than we have been led to believe and that they have an equal importance on the planet. I also know that each species has a perspective on life that offers insight and learning. By taking into account all perspectives, we view things with a much greater depth of understanding.

Our animal relatives are showing a rising awareness and urgency, to those of us that listen, about the imbalance on the planet. Their key request (or command!) is that we must rebalance, and quickly, for the good of all.

My calling was to channel the messages from the collective consciousness of as many different animal species as possible. The reason was simple; to share their messages with humanity concerning the purpose of their species, why they are here. To share how each species fits into the balance of the whole. Each species has unique wisdom and truth to offer, and when this is understood and integrated into our way of being, it allows balance to return. My life purpose focuses on helping to change the way we view and treat animals for the good of all. The co-creation of this book, faithfully translating the animal's messages, is an important part of this path.

So, with all of these factors at the forefront of my mind, I began to select different animal species. Tuning into their collective consciousness, that is, the one voice that resonates from the entire species, their collective wisdom and knowledge handed down through the generations. I allow their voice to channel through me, through my pen and onto the page. I am in a meditative state as this happens and I simply allow the messages to channel onto the page directly, unaffected by my own conscious mind. By acting as a conduit, it is possible to allow their messages to be translated faithfully into the written word, for us to learn from and act upon.

I thought it was I that was selecting the various species of animal, I later realised that it was always the animals stepping forward, in turn, to offer their messages. The animals "knock on my door" so to speak, mainly in the darkest hours of the night, just before dawn, I feel wide awake and hear the call from a particular species. I grab my pen and book and allow their message to freely flow onto the page. This lasts between twenty and forty minutes. After this download (and normally a cup of tea!) I fall back to sleep, awakening a few hours later, excited to read their message, as I have very little recollection of what they shared at the actual time of the channelling.

Sometimes the species give me advance notice. They start showing up in my world in different ways, physical appearances, visions, dreams, pictures, films or overhearing conversations about them. These signposts come with a message from them, asking to be heard, sometimes most adamantly!

This is closely followed by their visitation where my pen simply writes, often at very high speed, on their behalf. The animals realise that humanity needs to awaken and fast. Thankfully, many of us are doing just that. We are growing enormously in self awareness, healing our wounds and stepping into our authentic selves and true power. We are remembering the truth, so that we may serve our greatest purpose whilst in our current physical incarnation.

I believe enough of us will "awaken" in order to rebalance the collective consciousness of humanity. In fact only 1% of us need to raise our vibration to a certain level in order to affect a shift across the rest of the species, according to the hundredth monkey effect*. Remember, we are the youngest species on planet Earth. Our purpose is unique, just as each species is, yet we are the ones who are causing the dangerous imbalances. I believe, if left to escalate, these imbalances will obliterate life on Earth for some considerable span of time. It is also important to realise that this damage emanates from our core vibration, our way of being; it is not just about the physical actions that we are taking, such as pollution or deforestation.

Our role is to learn how to return to perfect balance, for ourselves, yet through our connectedness to the all, by listening to the profound truth that lies in the stillness of this connection. The precious animals have so much wisdom to share with us. I feel truly honoured and blessed to be here at this time, contributing to the changes needed. I want to assist as powerfully as possible with the shift in humanity for the good of all. For those of us with a strong attraction to animals it is highly beneficial and necessary for us to deeply connect with them now. We need to learn deeper truth from their perspective and to live these truths in our own lives. It is essential that we adjust our own balance in a consistent and effective way because in doing so we affect the whole. This is the most powerful type of change.

This book, with 44 messages, is the first part of what, I think, will become a series (Let's wait and see what the Universe decides!). I have kept them in the order in which they were given to me, as I believe there is importance in the sequencing too. There is one, rather significant deviation from this, an unexpected last minute message was given to me from the Giant Pandas. I was lucky enough to spend three weeks with them in Chengdu, China in October and November 2012 and their message came to me, as is so often the case, in the middle of the night, whilst in China. Following my return home they also made is VERY clear that their message was to not only be in the first volume BUT it was to be the very first message as well! Only once I had agreed to this did their incessant dreamtime messages cease! I can understand why their message needs to be first, enjoy absorbing their energy and wisdom.

I will continue to gather as many animal species' messages as want to contribute. My aim is to allow as many people to read, understand and benefit from these messages as possible.

One thing is certain, the animals are very keen to assist, as are all forms of life, they are stepping forward with more information at this incredible time on planet Earth. For those of us ready to hear their messages, our responsibility is to listen, to act on the wisdom and to share it as widely as we can. What happens, in our personal evolution, as we move forward is up to each of us to shape, our choices and actions are always in our hands.

Ways to Use This Book

There are many ways you can access the teachings of the species in this volume. I wanted to offer some suggestions though, so here are a few options. I'm sure you'll find others too!

As a reference book – If you come across signs, for example, a particular species keeps showing up in your life, in whatever way, physically, in dreams, in books, films etc. It feels like a non-coincidence. So look up the animal and read their message to humanity, it will no doubt give you important information and teachings for your own spiritual development and evolution. If the animal is not in this book please do seek meaning elsewhere, such as Ted Andrews' wonderful Animal Wisdom book or simply search the internet for the spiritual meanings of the species in question.

Intuitive Guidance - Holding the book closed, take a moment to connect in with your higher power and ask for guidance. Then open the book up at "random" and read the message. If it happens to open in between species, simply notice which page your eye fell on first or the page which draws you in naturally.

Power Animals - If you have meditated/enquired about your current power animals you can read their messages for additional guidance in your life. Remember, our power animals do shift and change, as we do.

Read the whole book! Simply read cover to cover, the messages are very powerful individually, yet become heightened when read as a collective, no surprise there then!

Other methods – Come up with other ways of working with the book and get in touch to let me know!

Perhaps you have great methods that I can share with others in the next edition/future volumes, to benefit all our development.

Please share these teachings as far and wide as you can, by living them as fully as you possibly can. "Be the change you wish to see in the world" as Mahatma Ghandi once said.

Enjoy the messages from the animals, savour them, digest them and assimilate them into your being and way of being, as we are all one in truth so we are part of them as they are part of us.

Love, peace and blessings,

Julie Lines
Founder of Voice of the Animals, Co-Founder of Awakening to Animals and Co-Creator of The Purpose of Species

* Hundredth monkey effect - The story of the hundredth monkey effect was published in the foreword to Lawrence Blair's Rhythms of Vision in 1975, based on his knowledge of a Japanese scientific study of Macaque monkeys that suggested when sufficient monkies on one island changed a pattern of behaviour, monkies on other islands also began to adopt this new behaviour. Also, Ken Keyes, Jr. published a later book called The Hundredth Monkey. In essence it too suggests that when a minimum of 1% of a population changes a pattern it causes a knock on effect to the rest, regardless of the location or the conscious awareness of the individuals

GIANT PANDA

Benevolence - A force of benevolence that is akin to all you will ever see or feel. Love of a level so deep and profound you can only feel joy and humble awakening.

Polarities are never truth. Only balance is truth. The things that seem possible are indeed that. You only need to allow it for it to transpire. Align your sense of worth to your feelings of worthiness and love for yourself and all things, and your dreams will become manifest, like a Lotus flower unfurling.

We Panda Bears come forward to you in this way right now as a symbol of hope in a world full of doubt and negativity. We come as ambassadors of light and truth and desire for you to share with all how much we need to release feelings of unworthiness, feelings that make us small or insignificant and to know that we are always whole and complete.

We stand in our benevolent power seeking you to stand in yours. Stand firmly rooted in your tree, your connection to earth and all, through your feet. Yet be loose and flexible, go with whatever comes your way and embrace all with hope and awe, reverence and gratitude. Know that you are divine source and worthy as an equal. Dispel any fear or judgement. You know your divine path, only you can. No others could as they have their own to develop and glean learning from.

Our magnificence comes in our connection to all that is, our total "beingness" of ourselves, we are who we are, it allows a peace inside us that no matter what, whether we are here in physical form or not we are divine source energy and are eternal.

All changes, the cycles of life and love run through patterns that are natural and aligned. Earthquakes, floods, tsunamis, typhoons are all natural things, it is only humanity that has forgotten these truths and sought to deny nature it's ways of cycle and movement. You must go with the cycles and movement, for only resistance of this movement creates blockages and flows to stagnate. Stagnation brings deterioration and mind made madness ensues.

Come to peace with us. Be peace with us. Take a breath and feel for stillness, peace, at the core of all your "beingness". We will see you there and dance together in a celebration of Universal unity and balance. The harmony of love and light with the dark of deep inner creation and diversity melds together to create a dynamic, spontaneous, moving, evolving energy that pulses through us.

Do not mistake inactivity as laziness, as you call it. There is much to be created in stillness and change emanates from stillness. Without it fluidity and flow is always limited. A time for stillness, a time for dynamic, graceful, flowing action. Honour this cycle of exchange and you will find us beside you, with you, as you. As one with you and all of nature, all of Universal energy and in this balance true benevolent power is attained.

Peace, harmony, united balance to and for all. The Pandas.

I channeled this message on 28th October 2012 whilst in Chengdu, China.

The Purpose Of Species

ORANG-UTANS

If a tree falls and no one hears it, does it make a sound? If the forests burn and you cannot see, hear or feel it does it happen? Does it matter? Look into our eyes and you can find the answers, look into your own eyes and you'll see it's the same. We are the same.

Will it make any difference if we are no more? Will it change our world if the fires continue to rage? Will it be at the back of your mind? Pushed away? When we are gone from this space will you notice? Will you realise what is the truth of this loss?

When the beauty is only scar tissue and desolation will it make you see?

We will not fight, we will not campaign, we will not moan or whinge or complain. We will simply withdraw. We will cease to be in this place. Balance is a fine line, all serves the whole, the whole serves all, magnificent is the whole in balance, unpredictable and savage is the imbalance. As hate is to love.

Bring love back as the centre, the core. What harm you cause to any, you cause to yourselves. Lost in the sea of noise your kind still pushes for more, more, more, never enough. Why isn't enough, enough? Greed and fear feed this black of negativity. There are those of you that see this knowing, feel it, hear it, know it. The numbers of you are rising, you can sense this too. Use this rise intelligently, one hundred monkeys, yes? Use it swiftly, accurately, wisely and definitely. Yes?

From within you sense this shift; you sense it yet may still be afraid of expressing the knowledge. Trust it's safe and trust you are never alone. Stand with us, as us, and know there is enough.

When you see us as you, as all, you know the truth. Only then can you appreciate the intricacy of the grand design, the dependencies and interdependencies of the entirety. How stunningly brilliant it all is, how precious and fragile the balance is. How glorious the masterpiece is when it is seen and experienced in the way of the truth. We are not afraid of what you call death. We know its vibration. We know its call and we flow with it. We are saddened by the hate and fear and vibration of aggravation that still attacks our homes, our babies, our friends, our lives. We are saddened that this is its brutal truth and yet we hope, always hope, you will turn in time, the vibration lifts in time, to realise the way, to know the error of the old low noise, the illusion of the old world. We embrace and want to be a part of the physical world, here and now, yet we do not resist or as you say "fight". We yield to what is, we breathe and accept. We have much to teach you if you will be willing. How wise our elders are and how we honour this. How well our youngsters live for the moment, play in joy and always yield to what is. How we care for each other and tolerate no infringement of our boundaries, our codes of honour and love.

We stand, swing, groom, eat, play, sleep, protect and travel with only love, with only truth of who/what/why we are. We want you to learn these powerful messages from us. We want you to know the real from the illusion. Will you listen? Will you hear? Will you hear the trees falling? Will you feel the burning, the destruction, the dying, the loss? Will you? We trust and observe.

The Purpose Of Species

CATS

Power in form, perfectly balanced. Effortless poise and readiness. Readiness for everything.

Intention honours our actions. Actions honour our intentions.

Perfect power, prowess and pride. Honour of ourselves, to our world.

We are light takers. We are bound to this. It is our divine role. We know when and who and where. We journey for a moment with their departing soul. Whoooooooosssssssshhhhhh!!!

Wow, such a rush it is! We are granted permission to be light takers. It is transitional, not bad or wrong or cruel. It is life and life is death, as death is life. We take as directed, as our inner knowing guides us. We take where it's just required.

You take in ways not divinely directed. You take in dark ways, troubled ways. You create mind made reasons of no sense or purpose, fake power or control that holds no energy, just darkness. You take too much, too many, too often. You created revenge, justice, religion, justifications. Excuses and lies, excuses and lies. Your killing is so far removed from our light taking, yet you seek to make demons of us. You must shine that light first upon your own before sharing it or seeking to turn it onto us. We are pure and simple light takers. We are balanced, guided, light sharers and protectors.

Some of us protect human frailty; some of us stay very clear of your kind. Most of us are persecuted. Many of us are treated royally, as we deserve. Much is needed to rebalance; much is out of control in man made madness. Our lives are always serving in divine guidance.

How do you do this? Look inside and know the truth. Step with us a while. Silent stalking, walking, playing, feel our soft fur, our paws, our claws. See our magical eyes and know we are mystical ones who understand far more about the way of things than you do.

You are in a state of amnesia, numb and lifeless. You can learn from us by noticing our aliveness, our vibrancy, our balance and self nurturing. Our purity of action, thought and deed. Puuurrrrrrrrrrrrrrr! Divine indeed.

5

The Purpose Of Species

HORSES

As the rain comes, so the winds carry the spirit of our world to us, with us and through us.

We are one with the wind and move in alignment with its call. Silence is where we play our games. Depth is found in our eyes, deep souls for rich learning for those quiet enough to pay attention and open enough to hear. There is an answer to every question, there is a bending of movement that shifts any state. There is a flexing brilliance, a lightness like no other in the fluid, fiery majesty of an Arabian wind dancer. The pride in the carriage shows the divine nature of the soul, that blends and merges with the divine, on the breezes and waves of the precious planet's air movements.

Impoverished are those that do not hear, or see, or feel this beauty. Lacking depth and subtlety are those who will not allow their true souls a chance to enter a pristine place of such light and beauty, as beholds the divine place of the horse. It is the only place where true serenity is found. It is the best and only place to dance with the precious mother, our earth.

We always seek to teach and show, share and enhance. We ceaselessly look for opportunities to show you the way, it is our very nature to hold this out as our service to the divine. Our unique perspective allows everything to be felt, experienced and embraced in a single breath or glance, if only you are ready and willing to notice it. Those of you with heavy, busy, cluttered souls will never even come close to touching this. Those of you locked in illusions of control and dominance will encounter a very different experience of the horse. Those of you who are leading the way, recalling much of the stillness will be guided by us, with grace and poise, honour and love. Patience and persistence. 'Til you hear it, feel it, know it in your soul once more. Leading from your authentic soul, your interconnected heart, your true place in the way of things is what you are destined for. You are the co-creators in this place. You are the ones who are able to shift the passing of things, you can shape and focus and create your dreams.

Notice what you have created, continue often to create, death, destruction, suffering, conflict, pain and misery. Think what you could create with stillness, connectivity, love, compassion and control of your minds and thoughts. Conscious co-creation. Shaping our world. You have this power, we are here to guide your stepping up and into the light. We will use whatever means we can to do this as long as it takes. Listen to us. You must act on this knowing. Share this and tell many. All who are ready to hear. All who are unfolding, becoming, releasing the old.

We horses are evolving too. We will not tolerate what we used to. We will not stand for the abuse of the old. It is time (place) to step up and into the new. Our goal is to ensure you reach a tipping point in souls that are shining their light across the globe to shift the masses in consciousness. We will always do this until it is achieved. Our determination is unparalleled. It is eternal and solid.

We see the time when a crisis will present itself. We foresee great losses to come before humanity is shaken sufficiently to act. We believe it will be enough and in time (place) to create a new way of living in this physical plane. The time (place) is fast approaching. It is upon us now. We are ready and waiting. Poised to assist. Are you ready? Are you willing? When you are with us ask us to show you the way. Prepare to be amazed and delighted. Run with us, flow as we do, trust and surrender. Connect and free your minds. Breathe in the life around you. Be still and vibrantly alive. Breathe in every drop. The rest you have to experience. It can not be explained. Trust and surrender. Trust and surrender.

The Purpose Of Species

BEARS

Light is in the eye of the beholder. Why is it when you look at bears you cast negative views like brutal, aggressive, dangerous, scary, man killing monsters?

If you see this when you look at us you see yourself, your own kind in this light - in this mirror.

Those humans who see this expect us to be like this! You get what you expect.

Bears, we are full of honour, integrity to our codes, fearsome protectors of our young, of our sacred boundaries. We live our morals no matter what. No matter what.
A judgment made is a challenge to undo.

We are nobles. Royal heritage and regal lines. We stand up for that which is important, we will fight for what we believe in.

But as often as we can we are gentle, quiet souls, who take what's needed in a respectful way and nurture our own in gentle, loving ways.

We share and teach our stories, morals and codes, alongside skills of survival and protection.

We build courage by gifting youngsters with challenges to attain. We build confidence by giving enough of a challenge, yet never too much.

We sleep in the cold, renewal months. We close down and settle into the deep stillness as we let the freeze take its path and in time come to thaw.

We slow, slow, slow, slow our heartbeat, our thoughts, our very essence.

We let the process occur in perfect trust and faith. We allow it in. It's all as it's meant to be.

Times for stillness are followed by times for activity, movement and vigour.

The Purpose Of Species

SHEEP

Purest love, light and devotion. Gentle power, so gentle yet firm if needs be, we work together, play together, stick together. Help each other, search each other, blend and merge together, dance together.

We are a thousand eyes of gentle familiar love, family gatherings under shady trees in summer months, together tight and snug in colder climes and times.

We adore our family, our own, we nurture lovingly our new souls, our new generation of love and light.

We suffer at the hands of many humans, not just in terms of our care and handling but also in terms of our death, no dignity or honour. Only fear, negativity and panic.

Despair, losing of dignity and cold merciless slaughter. No souls merge here.

We are sentient beings of light, just as you are. We are here to allow you to glimpse this, to see what you have forgotten, to notice how gentle we are, to remember how it really is.

To help others around and knowing you'll always be helped by them. This is true family.

Look into our eyes, see beyond your man made label and derogatory terms for us. We are pure love, soft and true. We love all our kind with all of our heart and being.

What a lesson to remember. What a lesson for humankind to observe and consider.

How can you be so far from this? How can you get back to this? Now.

Power in numbers. Shared community. Love. Divine souls linked together.

The Purpose Of Species

SPIDERS

We watch you go round in circles with your minds and wish you would stop and notice the vibrations all around that guide and show you the way. Every fibre of your being allows to tell the tale of truth, dark or light, it shows the way.

See, feel or hear it, the guidance is there, if only you'd pay attention. Stop and be still. Listen with all of your senses alert. Notice the movements of vibration all around. What does the web reveal to you?

It will show you all you need and much more besides. It will reveal what you are vibrating too as you see it affecting all around you. ALL around you. It matters not if a feather or a fly enters into my web, it reveals itself just the same. Do you even notice them? Do you observe, feel what they have to tell you? Or are you blinded by the bright flashing lights of the radiation machines all around you? The noisy madness of your chattering mind, constantly driving you to distraction? Commentary on the unimportant. Why do you do this?

Do you know the difference between this mind made noise and poison compared to the pure essence of vibration all around you right now? Stop a moment and notice right now. What is the divine vibration telling you now? Things you call animate and inanimate, ALL? They all reflect a perspective, an angle, a light beam that is YOU. What are you vibrating? THIS is worthy of your attention. This is worthy of your mind, your heart, your energy, your motion and emotion. Your web is the finest of fibres, invisible to most and holding an attractive force, attracting and holding the very particles you energetically align to. You allow, you encourage.

Wealth is also a part of this energetic alignment. Do you allow your web of attention to allow plenty, or not enough? Do you place your silken net at a point of much activity (so to speak) or do you intentionally place it where there is no movement, no air traffic, no grace or gumption?

We are all here to prosper and grow. We are all here to expand and elaborate on our essence, our creative abilities and tendencies. Do you allow your creativity to shine out into your world, your breath, your fibres?

Do you vibrate your truth? Do you allow plenty to facilitate this creation? Do you believe it wise to do so?

Blessed be the ones who show the way. Look for those who genuinely are able to steer their vibrations to allow the vast abundance and turn it into force for creative expression. Match and mold your learning. Know it is your way of being fully in this place. Know you are needed to prosper and grow. All of you have all you need. When you notice the nature of the vibration you send out and adapt them so as to guide all good things easily and effortlessly into your shining, sparkling web of truth.

The Purpose Of Species

WORMS

Your cat likes to play with us, so the other evening we arranged for her to bring a few of us in to see you, as we have a message for you. She sees us and the birds see us but you don't.

They have good eyesight, but you don't see properly with your eyes and your senses. If it's not clear and sharp you don't see it or value it.

We are always under your feet, in the dark damp mud, and you disregard us. You love the bees – which is right – because they are beautiful and you can see easily how they help you. We, the worms, help you too, but you've forgotten to look at things that are dark, messy or ugly because they don't please you.

You need to learn to look, see and feel things that aren't so obvious, things that are always right under your feet. Don't just look for the prettiness. Don't just consider the black and white, but look into the grey – there is far more meaning there.

Take time to consider us and what we do, weaving and burrowing about below your feet, bringing life to your soils. The most mundane things are often the most important. Go into your darkness and depths and see what is buried there. You will find your truths and although they might not always be attractive, they must not be ignored. Be brave!! They will nourish you and bring you life.

Face your fears in the darkness, feel the slimy dampness that is uncomfortable and horrible to you. Learn their messages and lessons. Face up to them and learn to love them, because they bring you freedom and salvation. Dig up the mud, don't keep burying them, thinking that if you can't see them they're not there. They will fester and grow in the ooze – so face them before they get so big and frightening.

Pick them up, handle them, watch them wriggle as they try to return to the depths. Hold them until you see them as they really are, what they bring you, and you will learn to love them. They will be your liberation. Channelled by Jean Davies.

The Purpose Of Species

SLENDER LORIS

The earth is whole, we are whole. We can only be whole again when we treat the world as whole again.

The missing pieces are inside us all, we all hold the key.

The world is so beautiful. I am so beautiful, yet I live in a dark world, so beauty is in the dark eye of the beholder. It doesn't require visual abilities to know beauty. It is not about physical appearance or softness of fur.

It is about the way you grasp your existence, the way you realise what you are, really, that brings about wholeness.
You talk endlessly of healing, when truly what it is, is WHOLING.

Making yourself whole once more. I want you to spread this word at your talk at Bromham Mill*, tell all those who will listen, the key is that we WHOLE ourselves again (and that is not about finding, making or adding). We will make the whole planet whole you see? How can we harm others when we see we are all one?

How can we harm ourselves when we see who we really are? I live away from your world (in the main) but we are always connected, always one. We are beautiful, aren't we?

Please remember. Much is at stake. It is all unfolding and much is to be realigned and celebrated. Joy is to know and remember. Bliss is to feel the knowing, to recall the wholeness.

Look into my eyes and see the truth, we are all the earth, we are already whole, we are always connected and we are beauty now. Thank you.

* I was a speaker at an event called Awareness is Healing at Bromham Mill in October 2010. I called my presentation Awareness is Wholing and shared the Slender Loris's message.

The Purpose Of Species

SPARROWS

We are often said to be connected directly with Jesus. And this is true. Yet only a partial truth. Of course, we hold the essence of the divine inside our souls yet what you have forgotten, and we hope you are remembering, is that SO DO YOU!

So do we all. All of life is part of the grand tapestry of life essence. This divine dance of twinkles on the water, all part of the ocean, always connected and made from the same energy, the same essence, the same.

Yet we have never forgotten this truth and even when the cats hunt us and try to transform our light we never lose sight of this amazing truth. Death is part of the cycle of all things.

We are a part of all things and have all things inside and around us. It is a huge hologram, and we mirror each and every other. In what looks like different form on the surface, yet scratch beneath the illusion a little and you find that spark, that light, that divine essence is there. IN ALL THINGS. It cannot be anything other than brilliant, for life itself is brilliant.

Do not turn your backs on this wisdom. Turn and face this truth. Your truth. All is one. All in the plan have a divine plan. What is yours? Follow your heart and soul. Remember and embrace, love and bring light to all you are and do by following your path. Bring yourself into alignment with who you are and all else will right itself. We sit patiently waiting for you to remember this truth. We will sit and wait until it is restored. It will happen and, oh boy, how wondrous when you do! How magical, light and splendid. What fun and joy and bliss there is to behold. What prosperity and flexibility and opportunity lies in store for you to allow.

JUMP IN! JUMP IN! JUMP IN!

All is said. Many thanks.

I channeled this message whilst looking out of my patio windows at a small gathering of sparrows sat watching me. They had been visiting every day for the past few weeks, patiently waiting to be heard!

The Purpose Of Species

GIRAFFES

If you reach for the treetops you'll find you can surprise yourself with just how high you can touch. Standing tall, metaphorically, is key at this time.

We are here to show you that anything is possible, that when you reach for something, you can achieve it more easily than you think.

Long ago, lessons were learnt about reaching and attaining and since have been blocked and marred by beliefs that say; don't, stay small, be safe, too risky, don't be silly, be sensible, who are you? Who do you think you are?

We are here to tell you that these beliefs are nonsense! Complete and utter. Your birthright, your purpose is to reach up and stretch. To remember what it is you love and are passionate about and to take all steps and bounds necessary to have it happen.

No need to strain or worry or fret. Trust and allow. Allow support, flexibility, bend and flow with what you feel guided to do. You are not in control, you have to know this once more.

You can choose to follow, or to block. This is what we have control over. This is truth. The rest is illusion.

Be wise to this and take steps towards your path (your true life's love and purpose) today. If you don't know (or can't remember) yet, then spend time remembering what it is you really adore, feel really passionate about. This is your right, your ultimate goal, your evolution, your expansion.

You must flexibly step on towards this, leaving behind the old, outworn, rigid controls and shackles of the mind made control system. You must realise these do not hold water. They are simply there to keep you small. Stand tall and realise you will and always will be supported.

That is our message to you, Thank you for listening. Now do so! We are a part of all things and have all things inside and around us. It is a huge hologram, and we mirror each and every other. In what looks like different form on the surface, yet scratch beneath the illusion a little and you find that spark, that light, that divine essence is there. IN ALL THINGS. It cannot be anything other than brilliant, for life itself is brilliant.

Do not turn your backs on this wisdom. Turn and face this truth. Your truth. All is one. All in the plan have a divine plan. What is yours? Follow your heart and soul. Remember and embrace, love and bring light to all you are and do by following your path. Bring yourself into alignment with who you are and all else will right itself.

The Purpose Of Species

RHINOCEROS

We are strong and bold.
Yet we are so vulnerable.
It is a paradox to consider
with regard to all life. It is
so that with one action we
cause a chain of events that
ultimately shape our futures?
We watch and wait as these
actions unfold. We hold our
ground.

We do not despair, not even in the moments of choice when
some cause our death for money and the perception of necessity.
We hold strong. We hold our grace. We trust that light will win
through. We trust that light will permeate the dark so far that no
shadows will remain.

We stand proud and regal in the knowledge of our purpose. We
show that with strength and power comes gentleness and grace.
With force and weight comes fluidity and light, like no other.

We offer healing to all we encounter. We offer it freely without
expectation of return. We bring in the energy of power with grace,
power with light, power with majesty and honour. We desire
humanity, the co-creators, to recall our messages and apply them to
your lives.

We who listen and understand share a bright light into the areas of
darkness. Do not despair. Know, trust your remembering sheds light
far and wide, hold true to your vision of balance on our beautiful
planet. We show you how to hold the energy of gentle resilience.
We refuse to change who we are. We urge you to recall who you
really are and to be true to this grace.

You are all magnificent. Just as we are. You have to believe it to
see it.

Hold the light, the energy, the vision, the trust, faith and power.
That is enough. You are enough.

The Purpose Of Species

MAGPIES

Gather, gather, gather. We flock and gather. Coming together to help each of us, each of our species.

We are taking care of us by being together.

We know we are not alone. We can't survive alone. Our strength is in our numbers, in being together.

Don't fear us, learn from us. Be like us. Flock and gather as a species. Leave no-one out. Listen to all – they all have a voice. We make noise. Lots of noise.

We are always shouting to be heard by the others. We know we must as we all have important wisdom to add to the collective.

Don't leave anyone out. Learn to listen in all the clamoring – for the quietest voices. They have the most to say.

Don't fear others and their voices. Their words, thoughts, ideas and beliefs add to your collective strength. Listen to all. Listen, listen, listen. There is much to be learnt.

Flock and gather. Come together. Leave no-one out. Listen to all. Many thanks to you, Jean Davies, for this wonderful channeling.

The Purpose Of Species

OWLS

Wisdom is light. If you let it into your being. All around you are the signs and clues of all you ever need to be aware of.

Do you listen?

Do you see?

Can you see in the dark?

Can you see through the veil of illusion?

Watch out, pay attention for the clues of the moment, the instance of insight that can turn any situation around into magical manifestations.

Busy, busy, busy, noisy madness. Fools are those who let noise block out any chance of understanding and knowing the truth. Your brain is of use, yes, but only to a degree. Out of balance you miss so much.

Trust your heart and soul, trust your gut feelings and follow through with wise action. Like we do with our prey, we wait, oh so quietly and patiently, observing, feeling, reading the situation, gathering signs, movement, smells, sounds, feelings.

Then let this trust guide you on the wing, swift, sure, certain, dynamic, fluid movement towards the object of your focus (mouse). Swoop, grab, take and know it was perfectly balanced. Look out into the darkness to know it is only the illusion. If you look with all your senses you get all the information you will ever need. Search with patience. Be still to detect your next need for motion. Act like lightning when the signs all show.

You will hit your target every time. You blend and merge stillness with decisive, guided action. Power is in this blend.

The Purpose Of Species

WOLVES

Hunting alone is not possible for us. We would not survive. We know the importance of working together, relying on each other. Trusting each other. We know how to create our larger self, our pack that moves as one. We follow laws of our kind, passed on from generation to generation to assure our survival.

What do you do in your world? We observe that you have forgotten much.

You stand, isolated and neglect the laws of life. You expect your life to come to you and to be owed your survival. We generalise here to demonstrate our concern.

When and what has to occur for you to recall the need to work together, to stick with your like and to create what you want? Can you rely on others? Can you rely on yourself? Do you know what you are hunting? Do you know why?

What drives you to aspire to this respect of life and all it offers? What has to alter for you to remember the truth of the reasons you are here?

We have at the heart of all we do the strongest, keenest sense of why we are here. What we are about. What our purpose is. We put all our focus and attention on this. We act from this knowing. Do not waste your time in this plane. Do not deny these truths a moment longer. What is your place here?

What are you needed to be doing? How can you make it so? We are crystal clear. There are no doubts, no hesitation, no fear, no confusion.

What about you?

The Purpose Of Species

MICE

Of Mice and Men! Indeed!

We have much to teach humanity about how to behave and how to be courageous about your choices!

We are said, by you, to be scared and timid. There are times when it is wise and important to move out of reach. To remove ones self to a place others can not get to. There are other times when we will stand our ground and defend ourselves and our own without hesitation.

We love our lives. We relish every moment. Savour its joy and energy. We are so grateful for every scrap of food we yield to, every warm hole we find to make our homes, every new dawn we open our eyes to. Every adventure and passing experience we behold and enjoy. Do you?

We see you in a stupor, oblivious to much, distracted and often negative by the barrage of news and distorted logic you convince each other is true. Demanding more and giving less.

Wanting more, more, more, yet never satisfied or accepting abundance.

We wish that you alter this mindset. We wish you whole once more. We wish you balance, grace and gratitude, blissful days, weeks, months and years.

We hold our virtues as ones you could get so much from. Gratitude, love, acceptance, presence, loyalty, remembering, sharing, allowing, receiving, protecting. Honouring. Revering. Being.

From these followings you will experience a way of being you would declare new, yet in the truest sense it is all there has ever been. We ask you to see beyond your beliefs. About mice and men and all things. Reveal to yourselves how things really are.

The truth. You will be in awe and you will be happy and content. As we are. Blessings to you, humanity.

The Purpose Of Species

KANGEROOS

Working with the force of this great Universe makes everything flow easily and bountifully.

Think of our kind bounding across the flat lands effortlessly with speed, power and grace. We are strong, energetic, boundless and free to bounce in our power.

Our truth is that we understand how to balance the ebb and flow of life itself. The essence of all things, all energy has a natural in and out, a high and low, like the tides or our breath.

If we work in harmony with this we always have what we need. If we give in balance to what we receive all is deeply freeing, plentiful and abundant. We learn as youngsters how to hold the balance and to be so joyously "great"ful for our ability to give to the Universe and to receive from the Universe. Both as the bliss of being in balance with the way of things.

We observe in humanity much is out of balance. Those who give far too much and push away things meant to be received. Those who always want, want, want and receive without gratitude and without giving in return.

You must get this balance just so. You need to perfect this balance and be joyously and effervescently grateful for your ability to do this.

Giving and receiving takes many forms and is not about money. Money is simply one possible exchange. You place far too much importance on that illusion you have called money.

No, giving and receiving is all about energetic exchange and when you get into the rhythm, one builds on the other, a momentum is found, a glorious symphony of action and reaction occurs that is like the expansion of the Universe itself.

It becomes easy, simple, wonder filled and blissful.

Watch us bound out. Notice how we do this and notice how the out fuels the in and the in fuels the out. It is a beautiful example of what we speak of here. Absorb this truth. Apply it. Yield to it. Enjoy it. Be thankful for this. Blessed be.

The Purpose Of Species

CAMELS

We are known as the ships of the desert. We walk miles, carrying heavy loads. But we don't let them become a burden. We are upright and strong. We take our time.

No need to rush, we know we will get there. We love our journey even though sometimes it can be hard. We are pleased to be of service, helping to guide through difficult terrain.

What can humanity learn from us? Have you worked it out? You will, take your time...........

Be pleased and happy to help others. See honour in the service, even when it's hard. Feel and know every step of your journey - that way your burden will be lightened.

Stand tall, believe you can achieve amazing things, against all odds. Don't let your limiting beliefs become your burden. Feel a lightness in your hearts and all will become light. Love your journey - all of it. It all has purpose and meaning. It might be very hard, at times, putting one foot in front of the other, but really, that's all you need to do.

One step at a time. Stop, feel, reflect, know, love that step, that moment. Take your next step and do the same. Love every step. Be strong, stand tall, take your time and love your journey.

Know that when you help others you help all humanity. When you help other creatures you help everything on or in your planet. Learn to love all you do, all the burdens you feel you carry. Feel the lightness of each moment and love it.

Channeled by Jean Davies with many thanks.

The Purpose Of Species

SEALS

Do you live your dreams? Are you experiencing heaven on earth? This is our right, our legacy, our true reality.

Seas change constantly. What exists within them moves and shifts. The vast depths and deeps may instill fear in some but it should not, in truth.

The vast oceans on this planet merely represent the depths and possibilities of our potential. Our ability to be what we want. Humanity is here to shape the co-creative force on this planet. We are here to show you how to go with the flow. How to remember the laws of the ocean and how to navigate through choppy waters and circumnavigate away from danger.

We see the sea (HA!) as a representation of your creative possibilities, your opportunities to grasp and develop.

So much is possible when you become one with creative force. It is so easy to get into rhythm with the force of life. Let go, be one fluid force.

Ride the waves; allow your dreams to take shape. Face any fears as they appear. Float with. Trust the ebb and flow. Trust the calm, the storm. Know you already know what your calling is, your true passion!

All you need is what, the how is up to the mighty ocean to shape and sculpt. Swim gracefully, with purpose, playfully and wisely and you will have all you need, always and so much more than that! (HA!!)

The Purpose Of Species

TURTLES

Life is what you allow it to be. Humanities mind made madness seeks to control things it cannot control and doesn't control what it can. This is pure madness. It's bananas!

So when we swim in the sea we do not attempt to stop the waves moving as they do or regulate their strength and movement. We do not believe we can alter the tides, the seasons, the sun, the wind, the sand movement.

We focus our energy on controlling our adaptability to the shifting tides, the seasons, the weather. We know our focus fixed on these things yields great benefits for us.

We know when and where to get our food, when to lay our eggs, how far to swim each day, how to hide when we need to, when to be still and do nothing physically, when to move quickly and expend much physical energy.

Why do you believe you can change or control that which you cannot? Or that you are somehow done wrongly by those things you choose not to like? Why do you waste your energy and time being negative about that which you cannot change?

Surely, to act on things you can change is better all round?

Your mood, your action, inaction, your direction, speed, your service, your love, your breath, your essence and energy.

Take a moment to consider what you can influence. Take a moment to realise where you waste effort currently on things you cannot influence.

This moment may change your entire life experience. You choose. Yes, you.

The Purpose Of Species

DOLPHINS

Looking from our eyes we see so much conflict in your souls. Souls in their essence are designed to be at one with all things.

Joyous, blissful, harmonious life is the grand design. We understand the fall from grace and the upward evolution (or revolution) and wish for more and more of you to re-engage with your true nature, your harmonious flow and the wondrous place of high vibration where your needs are manifest easily and effortlessly. With your soul team living in a pod or community where you support and assist each other to enjoy a creative nurturing, wonderful life fulfilling experience in the physical plane. You follow your bliss and co-create what makes your soul sing.

Respecting all things as sacred and one. You live peacefully and in balance. You love and revere all the planet, all of life, for the whole is the one and the one is the whole.

We urge you to remember before we are forced to withdraw from this place. We wish to be of service, yet we feared you might not hear. We are now hopeful enough of you will reconnect to the grid of light, you will remember who you really are. What we are here to do/be/achieve.

Life is a stunning, shimmering ocean, full of a wealth of delights to enjoy. All that your heaven on earth relies upon is that you remember the truth and act on these things.

Your mind is key. Your way of experiencing this place is key. You must remember this NOW.

We wish this with all our hearts and souls.
As you remember (the way showers) all will remember, it is the way of things. Only one percent of your kind must shift reality and this is enough to effect the whole. Be brave, be dedicated, believe. Educate your minds by learning all you have forgotten. We dolphins long for your return to heaven, to your destiny. Ascend, evolve, cleanse your energy, purify your very being.

Love with all your heart and soul all you truly are. That is how it is meant to be once more.
Be part of something truly remarkable NOW!

The Purpose Of Species

RABBITS

Soft is our fur, soft we may seem. Our life is made up of many facets, though many of these you wouldn't really be aware of.

As humans you are very keen to see things as you want to, not as they really are. Many of you put yourselves first and believe you are more important than other life. You put your perspective on all you observe, which we find quite comical really.

You drive yourselves crazy with rules, policies, ways of being, what you can and can't do, who you should and shouldn't like, where you must live, what fabrics you put on your fragile skins.

We want you to hear our message from our perspective to you all. Life is in everything, everywhere. All vibrates with energy, life force. All is equal and worthy of preserving, as all fits together to create the whole.

We are all aspects of the same big puzzle, unique yet bound together as one. All are needed, integral; a part of the system and any part missing detracts from the totality. Without all parts, balance cannot be complete.

We know your purpose is to be creative, to lovingly co-create blissful experiences in all manner of ways. We share a love of co-creating with you. We love to "act like rabbits", as you would say, yet we are much more than this. We give of ourselves in service for the nutrition of others, including humanity. We do this with pride and honour.

There is no greater gift in service than allowing your physical body to be utilised for the sustenance of others.

We send you a message simple and clear. See beyond the conditioned beliefs. Remember how sacred everything is, animate or inanimate. Respect all. Serve all. Love all. Be all.

We send blessings and love and a sense of urgency to our message.

The Purpose Of Species

FOXES

Fox; sly, cunning, shifty, cold, killer, untrustworthy, trouble, tormenter. Descriptions humans often associate with our kind. Misinterpretation and fixed views cloud and distort your vision.

Look again with eyes free of judgment. Look closely with free eyes. You will see an ever changing, highly agile, fluid being of the lightest touch, fast and active, adaptive to whatever, whoever appears and creates around itself.

All the folk tales, all the old wives tales, hunting tales of how savage the fox is, is human made distortion. What you see/hear you can get stubbornly attached to, fixed in your perception. It is easy to point the finger at others and accuse them of the dark things your own species is doing with much less honour and reason.

Fox cubs born, many in a litter. Hungry mouths to feed. Mother must provide and she buries much to retrieve in stages. Multiple kills with storage of the bulk for later use.

Much is deemed human property that we need to survive. Much of our territory and natural stock of our diet has been stripped away for mass production. We search for our survival. Have you ever been labeled something you are not? Accused of being something you are not? It is very difficult to change humanities views. Our message to you is short and swift. Release judgments that distort and hold no water.

Revisit what you believe and check their validity. Learn to be fluid and adaptable like we are and you will learn a great deal.

Tolerance of all is essential, understanding of truth is vital to our planets survival.

Family protection is core. Relevant to all. Trusting again is key. What is it within yourself that you trust so little it causes you to doubt so much else, so many others around you?
Love is the answer. And you know it's true. Someone amazing wrote. Very wise indeed. Live it. You must. Let go of the old. Travel in your soul. Explore the depths, shake out the old. Embrace the truth.

Morph and flex as we do.

The Purpose Of Species

KOALAS

Listen or your tongue will make you deaf. An old human phrase. Do you understand this?

Noisy, noisy, noisy, your minds. Chatter, chatter, noise, noise, madness, madness!

How do you expect to receive guidance on your path? How do you expect to be guided by the many and varied signs around you, within you? What is this need for noise? For constant action? How does it, could it possibly, serve you? Well, we guess it keeps you stuck in a world of crazy, rushing, nutty, nonsensical dramas that stop you knowing who you really are.

Those who don't understand what life here is all about. Those who don't care for stillness are deep in denial, trapped in the matrix of deception and far, far from a world of heaven on earth. Make it your business (serious business) to hush your noise, internally as well as externally. Start small and regularly build up. What will you get, you ask? Calmness, clarity, hearing your guidance from source via your own inner voice, via our animal voices that you can hear only if you befriend the silence. We are always communicating, always guiding and teaching. Imagine our tenacity to continue relentlessly to teach you, even when you have your stereo headphones on full volume all the time, so to speak. For those of you with ringing in your ears, be joyful, for this is your direct connection to the angelic realms, you may hear high pitched streams of what you may think is nothing, when in actual fact you are being given downloads of crucial vibrations helping you to evolve at accelerated rates. Do not despair if you do not have this assistance, simply ask and it is given, so long as your heart is open and willing. Learn to trust your heart and gut over your head. You still use your head but long after your heart and gut has guided you on your path.

Much is needed to change inside your world. For you see when you alter your inner world you are also altering the outer world. For as is above so is below. As is within, so is without. We are macrocosms of the microcosm, yes that is the correct way around. We are not mistaken. If you don't understand what we speak of, make it your task to find out! It is time to take your path seriously (in the appropriate light, guided way of course :-)) and to follow your attention of creating a heaven on earth internally so that it is created outside your so called self. You see, all is a mirror and as more and more of you light seekers create this for yourself so it is reflected in the reality of the mirror of the "outside" world. Hold a state of peace, long beautiful times of love and gratitude. Joyous experiences of bliss, effortlessness and harmonious flow. THIS is what changes the world. How can you treat yourself like a precious object? What must alter within you to alter without? Do you relentlessly create hell inside yourself? Heal and create relentless heaven. THIS is life changing for all are affected by this change. We speak of this for if you do not do as we ask your worlds will fall and crumble around you. That means our world will crumble and fall around us all. Do you see?
You love and care for animals, yes? Then love and care for yourself first and all good things follow this. Do you hear? Do you feel that knowing?

This is of crucial vitale (Latin meaning = Life) importance. You must hear this and act upon this knowing. The old noise and negativity THAT will cause only devastation and despair for all of us on planet earth. The new peace, tranquility and positivity of vision, now THAT will make a heaven on earth for ALL species, all kind, ALL. We are all one. Love yourself, love all life. If you say you love animals and nature you MUST learn to love yourself once more. Do not close your ears and eyes and hearts to this truth. Act relentlessly now to this. It is THE single most powerful, most earth changing, transforming act you can humbly commit to doing now. Be willing to love yourself wholly, completely and ask for guidance from a power greater than yourself. Listen, listen, listen with all your heart and soul and then act on this guidance, wisely, smartly and openly, trusting it will take you on a magical journey of rediscovering your authentic self. THIS will change our world. Are you hearing this? Are you feeling this? Please. Do. So. Now. There. Is. Little. Sand. Left. In. The. Timer... Bless you, love you, The Koala Collective Consciousness. I channeled this at 02.34am on 10th November 2010. I thought Koalas were cute and fluffy before this!

The Purpose Of Species

FLIES

Our purpose is divine. Just as yours is. Can you comprehend this?

We are placed here to do many things. All are important, valuable and of significance. What are your views/beliefs about Flies? Where do these views/beliefs come from? We see much more that you would imagine. We see deep into your creations. Deep into the world of illusion. We fly about, we observe much. We have the "fly on the wall" perspective as you so aptly name it.

What do you think we observe of humanity? Have you ever even considered we would have a view? If you have you are of a minority. We are mostly loathed, hated, most try to kill us, swat us or trap us to kill us. We are looked upon as filthy, dirty insects that spread disease.

Can you imagine what it is like to be treated this way by giant beings all around us? You have through history treated each other in this way, which is quite shocking to us.

We can offer you the gift of tolerance. If you would engage us in respectful interaction. If you would send us love rather than hate. If you would ask for what you 'd like us to do with love and no attachment. You will be amazed.

We are souls in insects bodies. We are here for a purpose too. We also clean up rotting flesh. We clear away harmful decomposing meat. We do it in ways that you have been conditioned to be repulsed by. This is just conditioning. We do things differently to you. This does not require prejudice and hate, violence and domination.

What would your life be like if you and all humans treated Flies as equals, with love and respect? All life with love and respect. Respecting difference, tolerating others ways and purposes. Loving the souls regardless of the physical form.

Can you imagine this? We encourage you to, often. Thank you.

The Purpose Of Species

JAGUARS

Behold our power, for it is yours when you are ready and prepared to accept it. Power in this sense is about love, boundaries, eventuality, drama left far below, connectedness and wholeness once more. It is about true integrity to those values that are ancient laws. Depth and attainment is required to aspire and inspire to these levels.

Look into our eyes. What is it that you feel? What can you observe about us?

Whatever your answer is, is the level you have attained to this point in your education and evolution, you may not have stepped into this fully, yet your awareness is growing to this level, and you will expand into this awareness with willingness and tenacity to allow. The many truths of life in this physical plane are said to be mysteries. The great unknown, and with things unknown often humanity leaps to fearful conclusions. The truth is, there is nothing to fear but fear itself, of course. There are no real mysteries, simply a lack of awareness, or a lack of understanding and skill to rise to the level of truth, yet to be grasped.

We are all here to aspire, to expand, to create (humanity, especially so). We are all destined to raise our vibration in our own life span. It is most natural. Reach into your soul and spend some still moments asking what it is you are guided to do next. How you are guided to be. How you can be of service in the highest and best of ways? Listen for the answers.

How you achieve these answers will all depend on how well you come into your true power, how well you can master your real abilities, your true alchemical talents and manifesting genius. How rapidly you can release, let go of, all the old outworn thoughts/beliefs that hold you trapped in so much less power than you are needed and able to attain.

Many of the other species have spoken with you already about the urgency with which you attend to these skills and talents. This, however, is not about rushing around like a headless chicken, so to speak, no, it is about focusing your attention and intention on your awakening. Being dedicated, consciously focused on revealing your true self to shine for and with the rest of all that is. That is what they refer to. You would not see Jaguar rushing around in a panic, now would you?

Take heed of my message. Consider your experience on this plane. You are meant to experience heaven on earth. There is much to be done to transform your experience. Please ask, listen, and take guided action. In your power. Peace and blessings.

The Purpose Of Species

TROUT

We are the trout. Plural. Collective. We swim together as a body. One gorgeous, slipping, sliding, shape-changing body. We can be anything we want to be. We all know our own mind(s) as one mind. We are one. We know the connection, instinctively, intuitively. When one is lost our body is still whole. It is always whole. Sometimes bigger, other times smaller.

It is the same for the human race. You too have one body. One mind. Connected in all things, at all times. Amazing things you could do if only you realised.

Always going against each other. Wanting to be on top, to have the upper hand. Have you never noticed what happens when you compete rather than connect or collaborate? You might win (hmmm), but do you really? How does it feel? Does it last? Do you need to try to "win" again? It's relentless, isn't it? Hard work. Gets you nowhere in the end. And completely unnecessary.

Think about the times you've worked together, or helped someone with no thought of "what's in it for me?". It feels more right somehow, doesn't it? That's because it is. Success is shared, is bigger, deeper, more lasting and makes you happier.
So how about expanding this? Not just one or two people but the whole human race. As one body. True, you will lose some people, it's the natural way of things, and you will gain some too. So the body keeps on being enriched by new blood. Don't fear these strangers, welcome them for how they can help this amazing human body to grow in ways you can only comprehend in your souls.
Your one human collective body will change shape constantly in so many ways. Not just physically, but in ideas, thoughts, knowledge, feelings, emotions, and much else besides. You must practice how this feels as there's no doubt it's difficult at first. We remember only too well.

Be bold, daring and brave. Uncomfortable new feelings and experiences in your new wonderful body are the sign that you're doing the right things. Whoever said change would be comfortable? What's the point of that? You must really feel it to know something has shifted. We can help you, will help you. If you let us. You see the body is bigger than the trout body or the human body. Your body and our body can also be one body. All the species on this wonderful planet are one body. If you struggle with this idea, take it right back again to your own single, individual body. And beyond. Your arms might think that they are the most important part of your body, or your eyes, or your lungs. But they are all connected in you, they all work together. Each species is a part of this planet's body, each has its very own important purpose. None can function on its own. All species need all other species. We all need you, the human species, to join with each other as one body, and for this whole, human body to connect completely with all other species, as the rest of us have been doing for a very long time. We all need you now. Come together. Wait no longer, the door is closing, come in now and be one with us all. Make us all whole again.

Channelled by Jean Davies. Many thanks to you Jean. :-)

53

The Purpose Of Species

SWANS

When you look at your reflection what do you see? How do you view yourself? What words/feelings do you have about yourself?

Write these things down and ask yourself what this tells you about the world you are creating around you. Your world is the perfect mirror of the thoughts and feelings that you have.

When we look at our reflection in the water we see pure grace, elegance, beauty, divinity, splendor and power. Whether we are cygnet or swan. Yes, we transfigure from cygnet to swan yet we do not place judgment on which state is better or worse, more or less beautiful. We know all stages are beautiful, all is beautiful.

Many conditions are in place in humanity to prevent you from feeling like you can allow yourself to see beauty in your reflection. Many mindsets/beliefs are there in place telling you; " not to be vain" or "who do you think you are?" or "get off your high horse" or "I'm ugly, too short, too tall, too fat, too thin" and on and on and on and on...

Whilst you torment yourself with all this negativity you cannot shine. You cannot realise and release your true creative potentiality. You are trapped, held back, restrained, gagged and tied in shackles. Release yourself from these constraints and stretch open your wings, feel the power in your body, heart and soul and use your mind wisely to sift out the old and to embrace lovingly your new and true reflection.

What do you see? What do you feel? It is beauty indeed. Grace, elegance, power and capability. Where to next, beloved humanity?

The Purpose Of Species

POLAR BEARS

Cold are the nights and days where we choose to live. Far from the madding crowds too. Although many come to see us and mankind edges closer and closer to us and then gets so aggressive when our boundaries get blurred.

Our message to you is this. It is simple. If you can hear this. If you turned up at this page and you are reading or hearing these words: AWAKEN!!

Stay awake, do everything in your power to reach deep inside and remember who you are. No more excuses, no more beliefs of "I don't matter, it's only me, what do I know, I can't, I'm not good enough or I'm not deserving enough."

We Polar Bears never question who we are and what our purpose is here on Planet Earth. We serve our souls loyally, patiently, obediently, diligently and always in our power.

We hold the energy grids of light across the Arctic Lines. We hold the ice of fire and ice in perfect balance. Do not concern yourself if this doesn't "make sense" to you at this point. You will understand at some point. All you need to know is that we are clear, we know what we are here to do and we do it with all our might. We know it is of utmost importance and we honour our purpose and ourselves for it is divine and divinity must be honoured.

Follow your inner wisdom. You can trust it, it will not lead you astray. It will lead you to magical far off places that will take your breath away with delight. How do you do this? STOP. Be still. Listen. Ask. Listen. Act. According to this divine guidance. This is truth. You are hearing this message from many other species too. This is evidence of its crucial necessity.

Look at us Polar Bears - we are strong, powerful, gentle, forceful, loving, grateful, dedicated souls.
How do you fare against these measures? Are you a fearless warrior? Or are you lost in a thick fog of fear and doubt? The fog must lift. You must lift it. Look upward to the skies, look around you at all that is wondrous in nature and look most diligently at you and answer the questions you find yourself asking. Lean into the answers you will hear when you trust and let go of all the old nonsense, illusion.

Answers to all are all around. Action is easy when your awareness is fixed and faithful to these answers, in the form of guidance. Begin, continue. Be relentless. NOW.

Thank you for hearing this message from the Polar Bears.
As I channeled this, I was surrounded by a vision of the Northern Lights! How magical.

The Purpose Of Species

ANTELOPE

Be certain. Be sure. Know who you are. What you will and won't tolerate. Forgive all, forgive yourself, others, other events, things you don't even know you need to forgive.

Then get busy. Get busy doing the things you are meant to be doing.

You know what they are. Deep down inside. They always revolve around love and gratitude, your passions and talents.

Make a decision, right here, right now. To be decisive about those things that really matter. Be decisive about what things you refuse to waste your time here on earth doing. What would your world be like if you did this?

We act as one in our habitat, we make a decision, it may be a call from one of us, but then we act, instantly, together, in harmonious unity. It is a matter of survival.

How do you think humanity fares around taking unified, decisive action that assists and allows you to survive or thrive? For future generations to come?

So many of you are lost in worlds of non reality, electronic lives that serve no purpose, other than to hold you trapped in a snare, wasting your lives, like they matter not.

What would your life be if you could shape and fill it however your choose? You decide. Then act. It can be so. If you believe. Commit. Take decisive action. Be brave. Unified. Co-operative. Or you could just float about, aimlessly, wasting your life, doing nothing of value and nothing to be proud of.

If you were an antelope and lived this way, how long do you think you'd last in the physical place? Not long, that's for sure.
Be swift, be sure, be brave, be confident. Sometimes deciding to be still is the most useful thing. Yet making the decision and committing wholeheartedly to it is crucially important.

Please reflect and hear what we say. It is for all our sakes.

The Purpose Of Species

PREYING MANTIS

Watch. Be still.
Be unseen.
Bide your time.
Hold your position.
Wait.

There's a time to act, for sure, but also a time for inactivity too. We know the value of the stillness, at the time of waiting. We know it and we honour it.

Do you? Or are you even aware of the difference?

If you are aware, do you actually partake in the stillness?

We observe your "busy"ness, your noise, your constant obsession with doing things, do, do, do, do, do, do.

All things in balance. Time to do, focused and intentional, for the highest good.

Time to not do. Time to just be. Reflect, consider, review, plan, rest, refresh, reactivation.

Yes, you need to regain this natural ebb and flow in your life.

This way you will live far more wisely, effectively, enjoyably. Yes. Thank you for stopping to read our thoughts. It enriches, yes? :o) P.M. (We thought you'd like our initials!)

The Purpose Of Species

MANTA RAYS

Stillness begets stillness.
Being in one flowing motion
with your surroundings and
believing in your mission is
all important at this time.

Much is changing, radically shifting, yet this is when your belief is at
its most important.

As your experience of the world changes, do you try to hold onto
old ways of doing and being? Or do you adapt and change with
this?

We Manta have to shift and change or we could cease to exist in
this place/plane. There is little sense in resisting that which is. It
can only lead to suffering and trouble.

Let your memories of truth shine through and act with flexibility,
courage, self belief and conviction, for we are all interconnected
and so you are never alone, it is simply impossible/implausible for
you to be.

Let the flow of life become your goal, your skill, being one with
what is, accepting and working in alignment with. Glide with grace
and harmony and make it look effortless.

We know our numbers dwindle in the world. We want to be here.
We interact with humanity to say we are part of this world tapestry.
We are important.

We wonder if enough of you will align and combine to shift the
desecration of our species? We will see.

The Purpose Of Species

TIGERS

Why are we here, you ask? We are part of the divine holy order, just as humanity is. You do not consider why humanity is here, or if you do, not in the same way, for your collective mind chooses to transfer your own shadow onto the beliefs you hold about tigers.

How do you know these things? You assume them. Tigers as murderous, savage, indiscriminate killers, unpredictable and always out to kill or maim. WRONG!

How wrong you are. If only you were to step into our paws a while and see life as we do, oh you'd be amazed, transformed by what you learn.

True power is always coupled with grace and humility. Honour and faith constant companions.

Humans are rapidly eliminating our kind, either for money or habitat. We are truly the hunted. We are truly the ones living in fear and anxiety about where we'll live and raise our youngsters. Our power brings great strength to the balance of all things and minds really don't matter in our world. Intuition, feel and emotion are our keys to reading the terrain. We feel the impending end of our physical being. We don't understand why humanity can not see that for true balance we must embrace each other. Understand and tolerate each other.

Live and let live. This is for all our sakes. Power without honour turns sour and black. We see and feel how your grasp of this hovers on the brink of shifting, yet is still loaded on the shadow side. A world without tigers? How would it be? A person without fire, without passion and bravery. What would they be? We all integrate with each other, all reflect aspects of the whole. Your role is clear - Wake and remember the truth, restore peace, harmony and vision of a life that knows only peace, valuing diversity, knowing the system is made of many parts, each playing a crucial, vital role. Learn more about how tigers really live. We model a way that resonates deeply within you, you remember, you feel the vibration deeply in your being when you observe our way of being.

Much is at stake. You can choose to wake and live truth. We hope and trust you will. Honouring the truth of all life.

The Purpose Of Species

HORSES,

We visit again with a very specific purpose and message, it is very important that you act as leaders in your lives, now.

We, as patient teachers, have consistently taught our human companions how to harness their true inner power and how to use it in a balanced way.

By balanced we mean feminine energy with a touch of masculine

This means with a key aspect of your method being about how to co-operate, to work in partnership, to support and harmonise, to realise the importance of community, how to ensure the thriving of the herd.

We are certain that, once you grasp and live this truth, the energies within you will respond powerfully and positively, realigning to the shifts on this planet, the imperceptible (to you) shift in the position of the planet that has drawn the turning point to an ever closer moment. 2012 is a marker, a guide signposted by the ancient wisdom of nature's laws. It is a guide in evolutionary terms. Humanity is wakening to this. You must use this awakening and activate your true power.

You know this. You can not hide from it now. You would not be reading this if you didn't know it to be truth. Have courage, let us show you, for those of you that ride with us equines, pay close attention to what we mirror in you. We show you vividly your internal workings. The shadow and the light at interplay. Healing allows truth to emerge. All you need is inside you. All you ever could imagine is possible is within you too. Listen. Break free from all the old. Its burden will rapidly become unbearable now.

Beware ignoring this, for we often will mirror your energetic turmoil and resistance in our physical well being. If you dare not shift yourself for your own sake, surely you will do it to allow us to balance?

Ponder this message. Read it and absorb its true meaning. If you don't ride with us, go visit some of our kind, in a field or stables. Quieten your chatterbox mind and enquire "What do you have to teach me?" Open up to what you feel. You will learn much from our wise counsel.

It is time. Be fearless. Be sure. Be leaders. BE.

The Purpose Of Species

TURKEYS

Importance is very clear, you must know that being in the present moment is the place where all things are possible. We welcome you to this place and show you how very important it is that you stay here.

In this place of now you are able to free yourself of past and future ties, shake yourself free of old memories and anchors and open up creativity, free of future illusions, especially those of fear or lack. We Turkeys are excellent at this.

Yes, for we do not spend our lives waiting for the inevitable, worrying about it, fearful and afraid. We do not become bitter, angry or depressed, replaying any bad treatment of our forefathers and mothers at the hands of humanity. We realise this is the curse of humans and we come to encourage you to step out of this illusion, this prison and step into being here and now. Living fully, expressing who your are, loving every moment, every feeling and experience and being so proud to do so and to be you.

We know your purpose for being is different from ours, yet we realise we can learn from each others differences. We want to assist you in realising, once more, that you are far more when in the moment, you are able to claim your true power in this place. We do not fear our duty, we live in honour of our service to humanity. We wish for respect and kind treatment, grace and dignity, we wish for this but we do not resist or reject our purpose of service to human kind for subsistence, it is our honour to support in this most fundamental, physical way.

We salute you, those who lead the way in the matter of presence. We encourage and show you the importance of what you are doing, for through you all will follow. Through your front running the masses begin to follow, with following comes the change, the change ushers in the new dawn, that which earth is turning toward, embracing that which we must all do now.

Be easy in the knowing you are following the path of truth. Be assured and comforted by us, yes, by Turkeys, to shore your faith, especially through your moments of doubt when old energies surround you and tempt your mind into the old beliefs and ways. These ways feel so bad yet tempt you still to their familiar ingrained patterns.

Do NOT fear, you are treading the way, proudly, bravely, beautifully, trust us when we say this, trust yourself to follow your heart. All is moving in divine guided order. It is only resistance to this order that creates imbalance and associated mind made pain.
Stay freely open and loving in this wild and true place of now. Let it into your heart and love it. You will see we do! We will share it with you gladly and happily, if you will simply be with us for a while. Thank you for listening to us and we honour and bless you in your unique human path. Namaste!

Channeled initially by the Voice of the Animals Playshop group on 23rd January 2011. I reconnected with them on 28th January 2011 at 3am.

The Purpose Of Species

DOLPHINS SPEAK AGAIN

I am delighted to add a channeled message from the Dolphins through Scott Olson, author of Messages From The Dolphins. Many thanks Scott for all the wonderful work you are doing.

This is today's dolphin message translated into human language.

It is meant to be sung because dolphins do not talk to each other.... they sing to each other. It is their song to humans.

"Wake up to your royal destiny. The celebration is at hand. The party is planned. The candles are lit. Please come join us now.

We are so happy; happy for you, you're waking up the day is new. Yes, this is the time to be awake. A wonderful time to be alive. A wonderful time to be witnessing your human kind waking up to all that we are, all that we will be, all that we will see. Magnificent radiance, illuminated wonder. A time to celebrate together. A time to share. A time to laugh. A time to dance. A time to play. We are here for you, we are here for you, don't you know this, what else must we do for you to see how much we care for you, how much we long for you to wake up, to wake up, come and join us, come and join us now please, there is no time left, so many changes, you know what we mean, our earth is healing and so are we and so are you.

Our caravansari sari sari of dreams, of islands and oceans and lands is here for you now, unfolding its wonders of wonders of the ages, yes you are this the dance, the song, the drama, the greatest show upon our earth. It is your gift of life here for you now, served on the most royal of platters, your royal robes, your royal inheritance is here for you now. Please put them on, you are the kings, you are the queens, we have waited long enough, holding the pearls, the jewels, the wisdom of our souls. Paradise nirvana, heaven upon the earth, so holy the holy, the land, the ocean, the air is here for you now, please, please accept your gifts now."

After writing this I saw on Facebook that 60 pilot whales had just beached themselves along the coast of New Zealand. This is so sad. I felt something about their current suffering should be included in the dolphins messages with the hope that more humans would read this and be moved to help end their suffering. So I went to bed last night knowing there was more to share. And this is their next message. While asleep I had the worst nightmare ever. I dreamt that another man wanted to hunt me down and kill me. It was the afternoon and he gave me until dawn to hide or get away. I felt so much fear and ultimate terror. I was outside and as it got dark I found a place in nature to hide. I stayed quiet and still through the night then as the sun was coming up, I thought I was safe and began to move making very minimal noise. But he found me and there was no way I could get away. I tried to bargain with him and said I wasn't going to agree to this but he wouldn't listen. He had found me and was going to kill me. So I woke up feeling the deep fear, knowing there was no way out. I was going to be killed. This is how this dolphin message came through me and what they want to share with you now... their feelings and the ultimate terror of what it is like to be a dolphin hunted, trapped, and slaughtered by humans.

I am empathic and I get their messages through feelings and thoughts. Sometimes it is their joy and vitality I feel as expressed, and sometimes it is their current suffering. At times I am very happy for the dolphins. Unfortunately today, in this moment, I am very sad for their suffering.

The Purpose Of Species

ELEPHANTS

Long are the dark nights, yet the sun starts to linger that much longer each day now. We are turning the corner, the significant shift in consciousness is well upon us now. Are you ready for this? As the planet shifted on its axis, the poles shift their power to realign with the golden balance. The divine feminine reintegrates its all powerful grasp of the energies all around - showing us it is here by the occurrences on the planet we inhabit. The rains, floods, and fire of Australia are all powerful signs of the cleansing of the old outbalanced masculine energies, the need for the sacred feminine to take back the power needed to create harmony and balance once more.

To signify the new the ice and cold winds rip around the globe, clearing, cleansing, renewing the energies, can you feel it? Feel it inside you? As the planet shows to us the changes occurring, these too are mirrored inside each of us. We are clearing, cleansing much, readjusting to the new way. The way of co-operation, partnership, intuition, heart centered loving and living, harmoniously flowing and remembering the truth and honouring this with the service we provide. We animal kingdom too are called to assist humanity in this coming to pass. We are urged to interact with you, to show you the way, to engage in ways that assist you in opening your hearts and reaching into your souls to remember the ease, the joy, the grace, the dance of service from a place of joy and love and gratitude, the caring for all as we are all. The blurring of old thinking, old boundaries and separation that are now useless and must fall away. Egyptians are sharing a very powerful example of this turning point. NO MORE! They assert, firmly and mean it. The old dominant, masculine forces are falling away, the energy grids cannot support what is old and outworn now they must, they do fade away now. Embrace the new fully and whole heartedly, literally, for it brings great joy and fulfillment, love and peace, respect and calm, clarity of purpose and meaningful purpose. What more could we want? Loving ourselves, our gifts and talents, nurturing them, honouring them and following their call from deep inside us, gives us joy and love like never before in this experience. Connecting and harmonising is all important. What can we recreate here? How can we work together now to create our heaven on earth. That is our frame of reference. You see I am saying "our" throughout, yes OUR. We are one. We are all the same ocean, unique sparkles yes, yet all one. All from the same basket as Virginia McKenna (Founder of The BornFree Foundation) so aptly described it. Watch with elephants a while. We see that for every situation there is a way forward. With calm, assured, loving movement or non movement we step onward, with peace. We are squarely planted here on earth, grounded so well and yet so lightly and so connected to our mother source - we listen to our guided path and tread it as wisely, as fully, as wholly as we can. We call for you to honour this true path. We call for you to have faith and courage to break the binding of the old world from yourself, to let go of the shackles that now have fallen away, they are not controlling now, there is no power left in the old ways, of keeping small, hiding our lights, denying our lights. No, for the time is to bring our light out, onto the table, polish it 'til it shines brightly and use it for all it's worth! To change our life! To upgrade our momentary experience from dulled, listless, nonsense to vivid, energised, exquisite, guided creativity for the good of all. Pray for all you vision. Pray with open hearts. Pray, knowing it is possible. Pray for the highest good and hold this vision. You must honour this creative process. You must acknowledge your thought, all thought creates the experience.

You must remember, awaken, renewed and fully awake to this truth. Emerge like the Phoenix from the old burnt away ashes, cleansed and renewed and hold a light, so clear, so bright, that all is sparkling, all is balanced, all is blessed, once more. When you do this, know this, you are as important as we all are. Your power is a part of all power. Your choices are a part of all choice and these choices move mountains, YES! Take this wisdom and apply it. For all of us that are ready (reading this) are needed, urged to do this now, the time is now. We tread lightly but firmly on this world. We want you to do the same. Miracles happen. Believe.

The Purpose Of Species

LEMURS

Leaping, bounding, boundless, freeing, freedom, energetic energies of comfort are our guided themes to you. Effortless flow and wild abandon gives us essence in that moment.

Our essence is pure and simple JOY of the highest order and level, light as air and flowing like water or a gently blowing breeze of lightness.

We do not become stuck or stale, no we fluidly flex and move ever forward, bounding into the second with all our might, knowing we will balance, knowing all is calm and true. We are the essence of fluidity. We are the essence of non-attachment to outcomes. We are so fluid our energy connection is blissfully high and eternally fuelled. This connection to energy gives us boundlessness.

Gives us joy, love, alignment, ease, fun, lightness, bliss and joy. We love to be. Of course we would wouldn't we, with this experience of flowing life force.

We adapt and mold ourselves to our surroundings, we become energetically aligned to all around us. This way the flow is pure and clean. It moves with love and power, how easy to attain and maintain.

What is your experience like in comparison to this place I describe? Is it helpful to know you are meant to experience this just as we do? Different surroundings, yes, maybe, yet same flowing ease.

What is it that stops you if you do not yet experience this? What would you do if your experience were like ours? Is this appealing? If it is then what are you waiting for? Live like Lemurs. It is magical indeed!

The Purpose Of Species

SUNBEARS

"Timorous wee beasties" Burns once wrote and that may well be the perspective you may offer as humans observing our behaviours. Yet we are far, far removed from this in reality. We are highly sensitised to our surroundings. We need pure high energy around us and sadly, most of you cannot sustain this purity of consciousness to warrant being around.

We have to tolerate your contact in certain circumstances, yet this has a high price to pay for us as we do not physically or mentally integrate well with lower mind made madness, you humans seem, often as not, plagued to endure (or to rise above.)

So we prefer, in order to thrive, to be away from such energies. It is not a personal thing, we understand you may be offended and this is not our intention, simply sharing with you our need to sustain a pure, high, energetic vibration to add our magical rays into the cosmic melting pot, so to speak. We are a rare and beautiful energy. The sun plays a huge role in our purpose. We are helping to balance the fire and earth energies to ensure balance and a platform for co-creation on this planet. We ground fire energies and help to dissipate the strong vibrations so that the Earth can absorb the magical rays of energy for the purpose of expansion.

This is a very key role for the balance of our physical stability. Sadly, our numbers are dwindling due, in the main, to humanities over zealous expansion and a lack of awareness of the need for balancing natural elements. We know that our essence in the non-physical planes is always present, yet without the physical manifestation of our energy something is out of kilter, it can be lost with dire consequences.
When creating fire, take away any one element and you will struggle, without air, or oxygen or matter that will burn you cannot make the physical expression of fire. As you eradicate species (and not just the animal kingdom, I hasten to add) you are damaging the delicate and brilliant balance, the chemistry of the incredible expression of co-creation that planet Mother Earth is.

Do you realise this? I know that if you read this you do, or you are beginning to recover from your amnesia, yet far too many are still stumbling through their physical incarnation blind, deaf and dumb to the truth. Those of you that know, you must spread your energy as far and wide as you can. This does not mean convince others who are still in their cosmic coma, no not necessary, but you must honour the truth, express it in your life, day-to-day and do all you can to live these truths. To hold the higher vibrations of this remembering, connecting with as many others that know too, linking the light grids across the globe to enlighten the darkness once more.

You all have a unique part in the mighty jigsaw, so you may say. So do not play the game of being small. Everyone has the ability to shine out and speak and tolerate truth. To live truth and share truth far and wide. Only in the individual ownership does the collective exist. We Sun Bears hold an exquisite light, a converter, energetic transformation, which is key to helping all others, as all others have their key to offer into the whole. Remember!! Live it! Share it. Hold the energy and focus on balance, truth and love at the core. We all can make a contribution of significant value and impact. Humanity forgot (with intention) why and how we are all here. It is up to you all to piece back together the jigsaw of life. Play your part. It is a divine part and needed to adjust the whole. We send blessings and bear hugs to you all. Gently, firmly, with dedication, share your light for the good of all.

The Purpose Of Species

PHEASANTS

You must let go of judgements. This is so important. At this time. This is not some spiritual quest to be a better person for that in itself is a judgement. For what is "better"? Ha ha! No, fundamentally, what we show you is the impact of your vibrational energy as you extend judgements. Let us walk you through the ripple effect that impacts all.

You see someone or something and you judge it (let us take a negative vibration). You judge it in a way that sends a negative wave of energy through the essence of your being, manifesting a return of this energy to you in some way, to match that which you exude. You also send out this ripple into the universe which influences the vibration of all it encounters. It is like the butterfly effect you humans speak of, yes? Your thoughts become things, you choose them. The judgements you make of the negative energetic frequency begins a negative cycle of impact. On you and everything around you. If you replace these thoughts with positive judgements, loving judgements, you will experience a whole different impact, on you and those around you.

So knowing this you must take ownership of the impact you are having. Do you grasp this? Whether physically spoken or not, every thought pulses through our universe and impacts all.

It is the nature of things. Your judgement of pheasants for example, you may judge us as silly creatures who run under cars. We are so stupid, why do that? You may think.

Well, more is at play than you may realise. We are telling you to see beyond the old paradigms, to open up your minds and realise beyond what you call death is only more life cycles. Endlessly form, non form, form, non form. We choose, oh so carefully, when to end one cycle and where, to shift energy around us. We do it with love and gratitude for all we are and all you are and all that is. Can you open your eyes? Can you see? Beyond the human instilled conditioning? The judgements you hold about life and so-called death. Is it bad? Is it sad? Is it awful? Is it a celebration? Is it the end? Or a beginning? Is it unfortunate or fortunate?

The truth is, it just is. All that determines how you feel is your response to it, how you judge it. What ripples do you send out into the universe? Do they help raise the consciousness, or lower it? Do you even notice? Next time you see one of our kind, think about the judgements you are making in your life. Positive, uplifting, grateful, joyous? Negative, depressing, ungrateful, miserable?

Choose wisely, you will see how your life takes flight when you vibrate more and more highly. Take flight!

The Purpose Of Species

SNOW LEOPARD

The Snow Leopards welcomed me in by getting me to sing in my head "This town, is 'coming like a Ghost Town.....", The Specials" (Snow Leopards are often called Mountain Ghosts...)
You must heed our message. It is one of love and urgency. We who live here in, and of, the clouds see far wider and from higher planes than you do. From here we clearly see and feel the necessity for change on this planet. So we tap into and are intimately connected to the higher vibrating aspects of source energy. Our feline edge makes us incredibly able to articulate this vision of what is required. You must listen. You must heed. You must change. You must act. We are operating at the edge of the veil, we morph in and out of this dimension and therefore, as all felines, we have much greater access and comprehension of all that is unfolding now.

We cannot explain to you in terms you would understand. Suffice to say, as the earth turns and shifts on her axis, so too does all of life here. We have become more visible to you for good reason. We normally seek to avoid contact with human souls on the physical plane as you are destructive and fearful, mostly. But we must step out of the shadow now and give you a message, for the time is upon us to move in the new direction. So please, heed and consider with your heart, not your ego, all we are set to instruct you upon. Wake, open your eyes. see the whole. See what is real in this planetary illusion. What you believe, what you think, how you are, moment by moment, is determining the reality of the planet. Each and everyone of you are shaping the world. What vibrations you send out create what is. As a collective, you must shift from negativity and fear to positivity and courage. Strength and connection. All that is. Do you hear this, down deep in your knowing soul?

Do not belittle yourself and your power, this is exactly what you must leave behind. You must learn to know your power, to embrace your power and take guided action in your power. Your vibration, your voice, as it were, must be strong, vibrant, positive and focused on your purpose. Your creative reason for being here now, building harmony, cooperation and communities of awake, enlightened souls. Do not side step this truth. You are called to do this now. It is something to embrace, to enjoy, to be passionate about, following your heart and reconnecting to all that is. What could be more glorious? Shed all the old, victim mindsets, dependent, negative, scarcity beliefs. Shed them all. Replace now with heart, courage, plenty, empowerment, passion and vigour. But most importantly at the core of it all love. Love, first and foremostly, of and for yourself. You are magnificent, just as we are. We have not forgotten, you must remember and NOW!

You may look at Snow Leopards and see spectacular poise, pride, courage, beauty, wisdom, resourcefulness and spirituality, connectedness and love. Yet, I challenge you now to turn the light on to yourself and know YOU are just the same. We access universal truth, we access it by listening and following our instincts, our heart feelings, our true nature. You must do the same. We beings in Snow Leopard shoes remind you that the damage here on the planet IS repairable, it is possible to adjust, to rebalance right now. The key lies not out there, with others, with more power, more luck, more fortune, whatever excuses you find, but within you. Right now. Each breath we take we choose. Alive or dulled? Powerful or powerless? Abundance or scarcity? Live or die? Health or dis-ease? Love or hate? Day or night? Good or bad? You get the idea, yes?
Think wisely, be your true self. Stand in your power, refuse anything lower. Change your world. Change the world. NOW! Watch us hunting our prey. This will show you that anything is possible. Join us on the edge of the veil and get ready for the time of your life! Shed old nonsense. Enter the new phase awake, alert and true to the purpose of this physical plane. Expansion, co-creation, love, joy, bliss.
Thank you and see you at the edge.

The Purpose Of Species

DRAGONS

You may wonder how can Dragon energy exist? Surely Dragons are fictional characters that are make-believe? How much else have you been told to believe that you are finding not to be the truth? How much have you been told is nonsense. Yet now, you begin to know it is indeed truth?

Stretch your mind, into fully awakening, majestic forces are all around and on many levels and dimensions, some you can currently see and some you are yet to reveal to yourself. The veils are thinning and dimensional overlaps are becoming apparent to those who are removing and allowing the truth to penetrate their reality.
It is a joyous knowing and remembering.

That which is Dragon energy is most power filled and exuberant, overjoyed at the emerging knowing of the ones who are here to remember!

We Dragons exist on a plane that is not yet visible in the dimensions aligned to the collective consciousness of the masses on the planet. Yet those of you who are allowing, quiet your non belief, quieten down your noisy mind, be drawn to places where our energy flows forth, where the veils are thinnest, you can ask for guidance to find such places and be willing to experience at least our energy, raw and powerful, red and orange, brave and true. Our fiery nature is a reflection of the rejuvenation at work on Mother Earth right now, as fire and other forces clear the old away, revealing fresh new possibility for all those aligned to allow.

Look with your inner senses, ask for our energy to be revealed. Feel it in your heart and prepare to be magnetised to our presence. We are not as we were betrayed by old tales of ferocity and fire, death and destruction. Yes, we are powerful, deeply powerful, yet not as portrayed. We hold the map of rebirth and renewal, letting go of old outworn baggage and establishing pristine new energies of strength and vigour.

Close your eyes and feel our presence, we are close, when you are open. Wings, claws, colours so vivid, hearts on fire and magic from deep within the fiery core of this enchanted planet.
Yes! We are here, experience our essence, if you will, taste the power we hold, the power you hold and embrace the process of revealing Dragon energy once more on planet Earth, it is indeed exciting times!

New and old merge, yet all is at a much higher vibration, truth and wisdom applied to expanded states of being and experience. It is where we are carving the vibration into a broad recollection of the truth, shining and glistening, fresh and new like the Phoenix re-emerging from the ashes.

Take time with us, for we will reveal to you your need of Dragon energy integration. You will understand how it integrates into your emerging reality and be reinvigorated and renewed! It is exciting times! Allow, integrate, flow, experience, BE! We salute and honour those of you now opening to the many and magical revelations of layers and energies re-emerging now!
Awaken!

The Purpose Of Species

RABBITS RETURN!

We rabbits are noticing that human energy is changing and for the better. It is refreshing and invigorating to observe. We urge you to follow the callings of your heart and allow yourself the joy and flow of co creation with the divine.

Following your passions in creative ways is the key way to restructure your wealth of energy, talents and passion and it is fundamentally at the centre of your transformation at this time, in this plane.

Much old thinking has blocked human collective consciousness and created belief that you can not exchange pleasurable and passionate pursuits for monetary exchange. Know this is illusion, crazy falsehood designed to keep you shackled to your cage, pinned into drudgery or denial of your true creative genius. Take time now to know what your creative inclinations are, write, dance, sew, paint, sing?

Make beautiful creations and do it vigorously!

No excuses. It is the key to unlocking your true power, energy and bliss. What you create in this way opens doorways of abundance of prosperity in myriad ways, so stop old, restrictive patterns of dull drudgery and get on with a much more vibrant, joyous experience of co creation!

It will change your experience immeasurably!

Whatever your heart craves of a creative nature is nurturing and beneficial to your soul. It is releasing and freeing you deeply and joyfully. Embrace your talents and bliss now!!

Love and joy, the rabbits.

The Purpose Of Species

BATS

Transformation requires the combination of trust, inner vision and courage. You are a creature destined to transform by your very nature, yet you seem to resist this transformation which, to us bats, we find concerning and confusing.

We know what we search for, we lock onto it and move swiftly and confidently forward, sideward, upward, downward to find our desires.

We are creatures of the dark. That doesn't mean bad as humans often label, oh no, we are receptive and able to create and thrive whilst navigating our way fearlessly through the silent unknowing. We urge humanity, you, at this time, to become sure of your target, lock your senses onto it and trust with all your heart that you will be guided toward that which you desire, set aside your mind made fears and fly with all your ability towards your hearts desire.

In order to evolve and raise your vibration you must transcend the lower petty mindsets and beliefs of fear, scarcity and unworthiness. You are an equal on this plane. Destined for greatness. If you will only lean in and trust this. You are woven into the great web of life and the illusion of separation, control and lack are mistaken thinking that serve no good purpose.

Much is to be shifted on planet earth right now. Bats urge you to embrace your inner wisdom, to trust as you fly into the dark, knowing you can rely on the support of the Universe and soar towards your real reasons for being here.

Look for us as signs to support you, we are around, if you only still yourself and open yourself.

As you open up to seeing us you also open up your knowing of your true life purpose. Grab this knowing and choose to act on all things guided from your heart to allow this purpose to manifest beautifully in your life.

Be swift. Be sure. Be focused and trust your inner vision and guidance. Do this NOW. The time is NOW.

With love and support from us Bats.

The Purpose Of Species

ABOUT THE AUTHOR

Julie Lines founded Voice of the Animals in 2009 and is one of the UK's most respected animal communicators. She is also a co-founder of the Awakening to Animals International Conferences.

Julie regularly appears as a columnist and expert in the international Horsemanship magazine and has a large and passionate social media following, where she is committed to raising awareness about the importance of animals/all life and how their teachings can greatly assist humanities evolution, for the good of all.

She spent many years, of her former career, travelling the world as a recognised expert in the field of leadership and personal development in the corporate world. This combination of knowledge, skills and experience gives Julie a unique ability to faithfully translate messages from the animals whilst also being able to guide people to in making transpersonal leaps in their own evolution. Julie is also currently training as a student of The Healing Trust, is attuned to level 2 Reiki and is a student Zero Balancing Practitioner, she is developing her skills as a new healer so that she can share more of the animals wisdom and knowing around the area of rebalancing.

Her services include; International Educational Conferences, Playshops, Equine Retreats, One to One Consultations as well as writing and co-creating books, including The Purpose of Species. Learn more about Julie and the services she offers at http://voiceoftheanimals.org.uk

INDEX

The Purpose Of Species

THANKS AND CREDITS

Artwork and Images:

A huge thank you to all of the people listed below, Liz for her stunning award winning art work. Thank you to all of you, amazing photographers for permission to use your wonderful images, which really have brought the book to life and help share the incredible essence of each species.

Award Winning Artwork by Liz Mitten Ryan
– http://lizmittenryan.com

Orang-Utans	Horses, Another Message from
Horses	Bears
Rhinoceros	Owls
Wolves	Seals
Swans	Polar Bears
Tiger	Elephants

Photography Credits

Cats David Bell
Giraffes Julie Lines
Giant Panda Julie Lines
Rabbits Nick Pye
Fly Macrophotography by Terry Crouch
 - onebigidea@hotmail.co.uk
Jaguar ©lifeonwhite.com
Antelope IMG 6550 Sias van Schalkwyk
Turkeys Yousif Waleed
Sun Bear Julie Lines
Pheasant Debbie Mous
Rabbits Return Klaus Post

Thanks to all the photographers of the following images from Stock.XCHNG free stock photographic images (names not available)

Sheep
Slender Loris
Kangeroos
Koalas

Thank you to all the photographers of the following Dreamstime Images Standard License Purchases

Spider	Worms
Mice	Camels
Turtles	Dolphins
Fox	Trout
Preying Mantis	Manta Rays
Dolphins Speak Again	Lemurs
Snow Leopard	Dragons
Bats	Sparrows
Magpies	

17562023R00064

Printed in Poland
by Amazon Fulfillment
Poland Sp. z o.o., Wrocław